T0129137

FOOD
for
THOUGHT

FOOD
for
THOUGHT

Analyzing the Process B4 Speaking

MJ

authorHOUSE®

AuthorHouse™
1663 Liberty Drive
Bloomington, IN 47403
www.authorhouse.com
Phone: 1 (800) 839-8640

Published by AuthorHouse 05/13/2015

ISBN: 978-1-5049-1251-8 (sc)
ISBN: 978-1-5049-1250-1 (e)

Library of Congress Control Number: 2015907749

Print information available on the last page.

Any people depicted in stock imagery provided by Thinkstock are models, and such images are being used for illustrative purposes only. Certain stock imagery © Thinkstock.

This book is printed on acid-free paper.

KJV
Scripture quotations marked KJV are from the Holy Bible, King James Version (Authorized Version). First published in 1611. Quoted from the KJV Classic Reference Bible, Copyright © 1983 by The <u>Zondervan</u> Corporation.

Table of Contents

Thanks, to you for purchasing this book. However, I am hoping that God returns the blessing back to you one hundred fold. In closing, I am empowered, you are empowered, and take action in empowering someone else.

This book is dedicated in memory of my loving mother "Ruby L. Mason". A woman that took all that was within in her and poured it into me so that I can be all that I can. In addition, she introduced me to Christ and said that you must have a relationship with him my child because only what you do for him will last. In closing, mom I miss you and I am grateful for the things God allowed you to pour into my spirit for me to do kingdom work. Love you 4/eternity.

Telling it like it is!

My prayer today is that we all learn how to love one another.

remove hatred . . . . . . replace with love
remove violence . . . . . replace with peace
remove jealousy . . . . . replace with rejoicing another's success
And most important,
remove self . . . . .replace with God, the creator of all things

Stay blessed and continue to think about it and make the difference. This is food for thought: It's tight but it's right!

The title placed on people called friend

We know that *friend* is defined as a person attached to another by feelings of affection or personal regard. Friendship on the other hand is defined as the state of being a friend to value a person's friendship. Loyalty is an element of a friend and friendship, and is defined as faithfulness to commitment or obligations. Personally, to be a friend means to sincerely stand by you through thick and thin, lovingly correct you when you are wrong, and loyally not allow others to discredit or demean you in my presence. As a friend I am the shoulder you can lean on, if I have then you have, if you're hurt then I am hurting as well, my respect and love for you will never change no matter who comes around or who I am associating with.

Now, things can get a little shady when so-called friends are disloyal and/or don't even respect the solidity that the friendship is supposed to be built on. People of this caliber are comfortable around others who discredit, demean, and damage your character. These so-called friends will "Amen" the negativity. This is not a friend! Proverbs 18:24 says, "a man that hath friends must show himself friendly". A true friend is always faithful and respectful to the friendship; defending it and prevailing over the opposition. In conclusion, remember that everyone you are friends with are not friends with you. Everyone that you are down with will not be down with you. Everyone you laugh with is not laughing with you but at you. The one you tell a secret to and reveal it to others. The one you sing praises about sing curses about you. The one you are rejoicing with is not rejoicing with you. My recommendation: Choose your friends wisely! Talk and walk with God. He will show you who is for you and who is not. His word will never return void and His judgment is always perfect. We cannot hide the real us from him. This is food for thought: Check them and disassociate yourself if the friendship on their end is counterfeit.

Today will be what you make it

It can be good. It can be bad. It can be exciting. It can be boring. It can be on a high note, and it can be on a low note. It is what you make it. In the word of God it states that we must command the morning. We have the right to create our own atmosphere. We are atmosphere changers. First, I gave God thanks when I rose this morning and asked Him to forgive me of any sin I have committed that violates His law. Then I commanded the morning and the entire day that it would be encouraging, full of excitement, and full of happiness, joy, peace, and love. Wherever I walk today the atmosphere will change and never be the same. Blessings will flow non-stop, and I will be a blessing to others. Hallelujah, my morning and entire day is commanded, my atmosphere is set, happiness is all around me, and I am blessed. This is food for thought: Now what are you going to do? Will you set your atmosphere? The Word gave me the right to prophesy over myself. Are you willing to prophesy over your life? If not, then shame on you. I am out to get mine. Hate it or love it! I know it is already done . . . here comes the blessings. I see them!!

Life has a lot of things we want but don't need

Bad decision-making brings about "The Haves and The Have Nots". Example of a "have not": If my salary is $25,000 annually and I am in desperate need of a vehicle, keep in mind I have other living expenses, why would I purchase a $60,000 car? I have the funds for a descent, less-expensive car. It can be managed within my budget without being strapped, stressed, or desiring to be someone who is trying to keep up with the Joneses, seeking man's accolades. The "haves" pray to God for the desires of their heart and give Him thanks for supplying what is needed. This is food for thought: This is a prime example of "The Haves and The Have Nots". I would rather have Jesus than silver, gold, or man's accolades.

Do you feel like the troubles in life weigh you down?

I am more than sure the answer is yes. We have to take a major inventory of our lives. Checking the parts we've played in our problems. If our part was not in compliance with God's law then we are required to get on our knees and ask Him for forgiveness. If you feel as if you are drowning in your worries, don't! Because you have a 24-hour Lifeguard and He walks on water. . . .His name is JESUS. We all must abide by His law, "thou shall not commit adultery, thou shall not kill, thou shall not steal, thou shall not bear false witness, thou shall not covet, thou shall love thy neighbor as thyself". Love worketh no ill to his neighbor: Therefore, love is the fulfilling of the law. Just food for thought: Let us check ourselves before we wreck ourselves.

Many us pray for money and
wish we had plenty of it

I am guilty of it at one point in my life. Allow me to tell you about the favor of God. It is worth more than millions and billions of dollars. It'll open doors for you. God's immeasurable favor is the key to everything. We cannot roll over and play dead and think God is going to just lay it on us like that . . . even though He can. To whom much is given much is definitely required. Example: in order to pay your bills you have to go to work. We tap into the source (God) and work at the resource (the job). My line of thinking is - in order to receive His immeasurable favor I feel I have to know Him, have a relationship with Him, study His word, trust Him wholeheartedly, decrease so He can increase, diligently work in the house of the Lord like I worked in the streets, proclaim to the world that He is my personal savior, know that when it comes to the only wise God that nothing can separate me from Him, and I have to wait on Him no matter what the circumstances are. But always remember that if you are ashamed of Him and His word, He will be ashamed of you. It is not optional, we must get our house in order, get our business straight, and increase our prayer life. Food for thought: Trust God! Man has no heaven or hell to place you in but they will encourage you. The choice and the relationship with God still remains your decision. What will your choice be? What a mighty God we serve with our destiny in His hands!!

I am just putting it to you straight again

Life has its battles, twists, turns, arguments, settlements, likes, dislikes, love, hate, discrimination, unselfishness, meanness, happiness, sadness, crimes, unsolved murders, and the list goes on for years. Let me put it to you straight with no chaser . . . God is still standing by. All we have to do is turn from our wicked ways, ask for forgiveness of our sins, be sincere, accept Him as our personal Savior, then the only wise God will take us as we are. I have no time to worry about the things going on in the world. I pray about them and turn them over to Jesus. He can and He will work them out. It's so sad that the Lord blesses us beyond measure and loves us unconditionally, and we don't give Him the time He is so worthy of. I am not preaching to the choir nor trying to pretend I have it 151% percent together. But, it is my duty and I do mean MY DUTY to reach back, grab one, teach one, and encourage one about what God has done for me. How He set me free, brought me out, and opened His loving arms to me. We cannot make it without a relationship with God. We must give Him more respect! Knowing He died for us so that we may have the right to the tree of life. This is food for thought: Check it or respect it. God is matchless!!

Death and a Funeral

All could be going well, but when the Lord says that our time and assignment on earth is complete then we move on. Death is the expiration of life in the physical with a transition to the spiritual. We decide on earth where will we spend eternal life. Death is something serious and we can't get around it ... "as sure as a man lives he shall one day surely die", says the Lord. Once death has taken place people mourn, and speak kindly about the deceased. Even though they can no longer hear. If you did not say nice things during their life, went by to check on them every now and then, picked up the telephone to just say hi then death is too late. Give a person their flowers while they yet live. Food for thought: Come to Jesus just now.

Strong Family Ties

When we are single and free we hold strongly to our family ties. However, when we become married some things must change and boundaries must be set. After God, your spouse and children are priority one! You have to take care of your household first to ensure that it is in right standing as it should be. In order to keep your ship (home) from sinking and to save your passengers (household) you must pay strict attention to the issues of your own before offering to assist others. With boundaries in place, it is alright to still hangout from time to time, assist others with issues if you can, and even give advice. Food for thought: Take it or leave; swim or drown.

Felt like telling the truth

Have you ever been in a situation where you felt like telling a person something truthfully, but you didn't? I'm sure we've all been there. If we say we love the Lord then the truth is what we must stand on, stand for, and speak on even if you have to stand alone. God and His Word is truth! Do you find it hard to deliver the truth because it may come across as offensive or that the recipient may not accept it? My take is that it is both. Because before growth and development, many people (including myself) would be upset when the truth was told. Now, I can take it because I can distinguish between the two, knowing when it is truth or when it is definitely someone's opinion of me and they're using it as truth just to say what they want to say, sometimes negatively. However, I serve everyone notice that I can take it because I am one who will definitely stand on it and tell it like IT IS. I believe in God and His word. I will not have a problem correcting others nor with receiving correction if it is truth. In conclusion, just be able to take it if you give it. Because the entire world is opinionated, but the entire world does not support or take truth constructively. Just food for thought: With the burden of proof being, what is your truth?

Defining Friends Mixed with Careful Decisions

Friend is defined as a person whom one knows and with whom one has a bond of mutual affection, typically exclusive of family relations. Have you ever wondered in bonding with someone, and during the good times thought that it would be unbreakable? Well, it is the little things that can really destroy a friendship, family relationship, and specific bonds. Little things like misunderstandings, taking things too personal, lack of respect for one another, mood swings, lack of consideration for each other's opinions, lack of trust, always dwelling on negativity, and no respect for another person's space without thinking that they are being funny because they took a few days break from you. If we are friends and respect the bond we have built over time (you knowing my character and me knowing yours) then we must be able to agree to disagree. That's what friends do. In addition, if neither of us can respect and consider the things mentioned and deviate from the pettiness then the friendship, bond, or relationship was never a solid one. Decisions must be made concerning the friendship, family relationship, and/or bond. If one of us has too much pride to ask for forgiveness and to make the first point of contact instead of waiting on the other then decisions must be set into action. If you do not forgive me or I you, then we have a problem. Sometimes friendships/relationships do not recover from something so simple. The friendship/relationship may have run its course and we must love each other from a distance. It takes two to tango! So choose your friends carefully. Move on . . . it is not that serious! Just food for thought: If we do not invite Christ into our friendships, family relationships and/or bonds then we are doomed. In conclusion, we must invite Him in all we do because He will direct our paths. Again, just food for thought: If the shirt does not fit then stay out of Baby-Gap and move on to Gap for adults! I am sure something will fit. Take heed!! Stay Encouraged at all times!!!

Do not forget . . . Deliverance is key

We all have made decisions we regret, traveled some roads we regret, and at some point thought it was all about us. If you were a stripper and don't strip anymore - - you are delivered. If you were a thief and don't steal anymore - - you are delivered. If you were a drug dealer and don't deal anymore - - you are delivered. If you were a gangster and don't terrorize people anymore - - you are delivered. If you were with the devil and now you are with Jesus and live for Him - - you are delivered. I have heard people who once was an ex-something now criticize and harshly judge others. Don't say anything or point the finger at them because your past is now their future and remember someone said the same things about you when you were in the same territory. Therefore, think before you speak and give thanks to God for your deliverance as you pray for the deliverance of others. Because that once was your present which is now your yesterday and people do remember. So encourage the people who are presently living your yesterday to strive towards the escape God has provided for them. Allow deliverance to be evident in their lives like God allowed it to be in yours. Food for thought: Deliverance is key.

Man meets woman and woman chooses man

When two people are involved in a relationship, be it man meets woman or woman meets man, and children are involved, they are part of the family package. They should be embraced, loved, and respected. If a woman meets a man with children that are not biologically hers or vice versa each party will be responsible for accepting those non-biological children as their own, responsibly assisting in raising them and teaching them right from wrong; and agreeing on the terms of punishment for the disobedient child. However, parents must not allow the children to play one parent against the other. If the answer is no then both parents must stand firmly on no. If this cannot be established then neither party has any business even being life partners or developing a relationship point blank. Just food for thought: Remember, it is all about the relationship, family values and pushing the children to be successful, functioning educated citizens.

A mover and a shaker

We've all been in deep conversations in different group settings . . . . all male, all female, or a mixture of the two. Let's say the topic of conversation is about the troubled relationship of one of the group members; some members of the group had no comment, some said what they thought was best for the "hurting", and there were some that said "pray and ask God". All of the comments at the moment appeared to soothe the hurting. If the shoe was on my foot, I would pay strict attention to the one that had no comment at all. Reason being, most of the ones who are giving advice and commenting are the ones who are most likely going through the exact same thing and won't take their own advice. At times it has been a known fact that the one who has no comment has been through it, picked up the pieces of their life, dropped the burden that was bringing them down, and moved on, and it shows in their body language. I consider this person to be a mover and a shaker. They took no advice and gave no advice. Somehow they carefully evaluated their situation, and mounted up with wings like an eagle with an "I can show you better than I can tell you" mentality. This is why they had no comment in reference to the current situation. This is food for thought: Be a mover and a shaker! You will come out better.

It's your thing, do what you want to do and deal with the results

We all have the right to freedom of speech and the free willpower to do whatever makes us feel good. Example if you decide to be a stripper, if you decide to be a prostitute or if you decided to be a porn star it is your thing do what you want to do and deal with the results of your actions. I am a strong believer in not passing judgment on another individual and a strong believer in stating the facts. However, if you are a female of color and you are doing things that degrades your character as a mother of children then you should think about your actions and how they would not only impact you but the lives of your children. Your children will have to deal with the comments others make about their mom, they get in fights because the negative comments makes them feel some type of way, they lash out because they have not been taught how to deal with what people think or may say, and the list goes on. Respect yourself so that others will respect you and your children. I get it! You are right, it is your thing and you can do what you want to do. But when you are raising minors it is not their thing and they cannot do what they want to do even when it is damaging to them. Show them the right way to the finish line and if they depart from it, it will not be because you did not teach them. If you decide not to teach them and live any type of life in front of them with no respect for them or yourself then do not be upset when their pattern mirrors yours. They are just a product of their environment, exposed to a life of no self respect, and mimicking and practicing a lifestyle presented by their mom as being okay. This is food for thought: It's your thing and you can do what you want to do! But do it with respect to display excellent leadership to your children.

Feeling like you want to crawl in a hole to hide from it all

Well, sometimes it appears like things in life can get totally out of control. Meaning, bills are due and there is no money to pay them, children getting in trouble and you don't even have two nickels to rub together to get them out of trouble, husband having an outside marital affair and you are doing all the right things as a wife should, parents have fallen prey to life's illnesses and even though you are praying it appears not to be working at all. You breakdown screaming that "you are only one person", "where did I go wrong"? You begin to question God and reply before He does by saying "I want to crawl into a hole and hide from it all". I serve you notice today that life would not be life if these types of problems did not exist. There will be no need for God or to call on Him if everything in life was perfect. The physical man (the flesh) is so weak and can only hold up for so long. However, the spirit man identified as the inner shell remains in order and holding up while everything on the outside is breaking down. The spirit is strong which is sustained by the word of God that has been imparted in our hearts. Go ahead and give it your best shot. Utilize the word of God, pull the trigger, and fire away at the devil and the situation. You will find out that God is larger than life and even greater than our circumstance. We must look at the situation with a smile and say "I made it" I am still standing. This is food for thought: There is no need to crawl into a hole and hide from it all. You cannot aim at the target and hit the bulls-eye if you hide.

Time is ticking so do not put off for tomorrow for what you can do today

I feel that we all live by a plan whether it's documented physically or mentally. We attempt to follow those plans and somehow we always do the first one and everything else falls through. The plans in my life I had set fell through because I made them in a spur of the moment. A moment where change was needed but I was not prepared mentally, and while in the middle of a conversation said what felt good for that moment. Yes, when the elements of reality in life struck and change was very necessary I had to be ready quickly, physically and mentally because it was all so serious. Too serious to the point where I was going places but not really getting anywhere. I was wasting time telling myself I have until tomorrow and I can do it then while living in the right now. But when my mind was transformed, my line of thinking was different, my conversations were different, my respect for people was different, my love for people was different, the depth of my heart was different, and even being effective in my community was different. Again, it was only one way and that was with God and for God. Allowing Him to take control. I was no longer putting off for tomorrow for what the only wise God gave me time to do today . . . it was never my time anyway. Therefore, do not put off for tomorrow for what God has given you time to do today. We are operating in His world, on borrowed time and it is ticking. So get the job done in the right-now. This is food for thought and I am just saying though.

Plagiarizing and feeling good about it . . . I dare you!

Plagiarizing is simply defined as to steal and pass off the idea of another as one's own. Living on this side of life we have seen and even known about someone who has done this. Once upon a time in life we may have done it and felt it was okay. Knowing that it was not our own. Even we are not our own and were purchased with a price. It is a known fact that people will steal a sermon word for word, preach it at another church, and feel as if they did a swell job. But, the thief did not realize that while he or she was up "going forth and really shaking the people up" with the stolen sermon that another individual was in the audience who happened to be at the prior church when the original person preached that sermon. However, this individual did not say anything because they felt it would have been robbery to steal the thief's shine even though it was stolen from someone else. God knows best and you are considered a fake. Be not surprised! Because the ideas of others have been stolen and the thief profited from it, and still take credit for birthing the idea . . . so they think. I serve you notice that God has given each one of us thoughts, ideas, and even a sermon, but many do not labor for it. Wanting someone else to labor for it and then plagiarize it to get the accolades. I call you, as well as myself, to repentance and will support truth and give credit where credit is due. "God, You are due this credit and every man knows this is Your doing. I do not want to be a fake anymore. I am going to activate what You gave me and allow You to drive this bus." This is food for thought: Ride off your own and not someone else's . . . I dare you!

What if?

A lot of times we go through life saying "what if". Things that the Almighty God has given you wisdom, knowledge, and power to change -- go ahead and change them. If He has not given you the "go ahead" then it means He is handling that portion and you just follow suit like you would in a card game. I want to name a few things that made us all say "what if": What if I had millions of dollars? What if I was in a position of leadership? What if it were me? What if I had more time? What if I won the lottery? What if I was God? What if I owned this or that? All of that sounds good because we all have been a part of that "what if" factor. However, what ifs are now decreed, declared, and has come forth in the right-now because we are to claim those things as though they are. I am a millionaire because I am rich in spirit and washed in His blood, God has given me leadership over a few things and made me ruler of many, I do own some of this and some of that and by His grace and mercy I am still here and have been deemed fisher of men. My word to the wise is never thirst after or become jealous of things God granted another person because you don't know what they went through to be granted that. Now, what if I fall to my knees, ask the Lord to forgive me of my sins, and tell Him "anyway you bless me dear Lord I am satisfied". I am seeking the Kingdom of heaven and everything else will be added unto me. This is food for thought: I do not wish I was God. The Ruler of all rulers said it best, "no other God before Him" and He means just that.

Things that have run its course

Life is something that can even run its course, so we must take notice. As we live on this earth things come, things go, things that are new have now become old, things that are fresh becomes stale, friends come, and they definitely go, because all have run its course. When things begin to change do not become dismayed. God is taking you to another level and everyone and everything is not meant to rise to that level with you. Yes, it may get a little uncomfortable and may seem a little weird but place your trust in God because He never makes mistakes and always provide instructions, but we don't always pay attention. Friends, say we come to a point where we cannot agree to disagree and we do not have that same love for each other as we once did; this means the friendship has run its course and it is time to forgive, forget, continue to love one another, and move on. Now, when life has run its course and the Lord says that will be all for you on this side of life then everything in the eyesight of man comes to a complete stop, the spirit has been removed from the body and now is present with the Lord. Again, this is food for thought: Nothing lasts forever, but eternal life. Therefore, give up placing value on earthly things that men are fascinated with and place value on your spirit as well as your walk with Christ so that you can live eternally where the streets are paved with gold.

Give it your best shot

Many times people do not want other brothers or sisters to be freed from the ghetto mentality. Today, we as a people are always blaming things on the Caucasian man for what happened back in our parent's time. However, we have not taken notice or given our parents credit for displaying strength through prayer and endurance during those difficult times, so that we will be free mentally and not become a present result of the past enslavement. If we have not advanced it is because we do not embrace endurance, and are too busy living in our parents past based on what we hear them talking about, but haven't ever experienced. Place your shoes on tight, string them up, and embrace your own life's experiences with determination no matter what it looks like. Say to yourself "endurance, I know I have it because it is in my DNA; defeat and giving up are not a part of my vocabulary or make up. I am a winner, a fighter, and a survivor. I am in it to win it (me and the Lord). I am going to give it my best shot and score. The sky is the limit for me and with God I always win. No matter what, I see the finish line and I am the last man standing . . . meaning I have conquered all". This is food for thought: I gave it my best shot and look at me now. My future is so bright - I got it and I am holding to my faith.

Church Folks who are perfect

We all have come in contact with church folks who have been free from sin all of their lives, made no mistakes, and God left them in charge to judge others . . . or so they think. Church folks appear to get the meaning and definition of hiding and privacy totally mixed up. To my understanding the definition of hiding is to conceal from sight or prevent from being seen. In addition, privacy is defined as the state of being free from intrusion disturbance in one's private life or affairs. Now, I am more than sure that even the perfect church folks want a little privacy to just get away from it all. When things become private it means that others are not a part of it only me, myself, and God. Being nosey is defined as unduly curiosity about the affairs of others. This definition really hit the nail on the head for perfect church folk. Be about God's business and not that of others. I serve you notice to pay attention to your own shortcomings because you do have them. If you don't, then you must not be born of this time. However, you will get a wakeup call that you are not at all perfect. Stop, look, and listen . . . sweep around your own front door before you try to sweep around someone else's. Just pray for people and for yourself. We all have stains on our lives, or have done something that someone else may disapprove of. But the judgment is up to the only wise God and not us. Therefore, there is no need for you to be in charge of my life nor my shortcomings just pray and keep your mouth closed and allow God to do the rest. Guess what? Someone knows something about you that you think no one knows. All of our closets are full of things. Take it or leave it. I said it, I mean it, and I will not take it back. If you are free from sin then you are granted a pass to check others. Somehow, I know you can't because no one is without sin, it just hasn't been exposed - - so stop judging others before it is. This is food for thought: The perfect church folk ought to leave other people alone, do their duty of praying for others, and drive in their own lane - - because life is not a one way street and I am sure you know this.

Speak and support truth . . . it says a lot about your character

In situations we sometimes use the term "Keeping it real" loosely. If you are one to keep it real then it will be done in all situations and scenarios. The Truth: we must speak it, support it, and live it whether it benefits us or not. To me this is called keeping it real. Speak is defined as someone who talks about something with a group of people; support is defined as to bear or hold up and even load or serve as a foundation to sustain or withstand without giving way; and truth is defined as the real facts about something or the things that are true with the support of a statement or idea accepted as truth. This is what strikes me with the "keep it real" people - when a situation arises and truth is revealed that rules in favor of who you deemed the enemy and you take offense, all of a sudden you have a case of amnesia. The truth hurts and you become angry when the truth is supported. If we are friends and you know I am totally wrong, do not support me nor allow me to think I am right. Correct me by speaking, supporting, and living the truth. I am still your friend and you are even a better friend because you sided with truth, called me on the carpet about it, and remained respectful while doing so. I truly believe God honors those who speak, support, and live truth backed up by His word. Now, if you waiver when it comes to the truth then this means to me you are unstable in all of your ways. Anyone who waivers or can be persuaded to support non-truth they are dangerous and I would be as well if I fall prey to the same thing. Now, I am standing my ground by speaking, supporting, and living truth as it relates to the word of God. This is food for thought: Speak it, support it, and live it! You will survive.

Pending definitely means undecided

I could look at my life and see a lot of things I have been undecided about. I have been undecided at least once in my lifetime about some friendships, relationships, communications, and even God. However, some friendships still remained undecided because I am not sure if we are good together or better apart. My relationship with God was undecided. But when He proved Himself to me without having to I knew then there was no more lingering. I had to make the choice to serve Him and make it quick. Then comes the communication that I left pending with family members and people who really had my best interest at heart. Now that I know better I am doing better - - serving the Lord, my community, taking a great interest in family, and making the difference - - my way of giving back to those who reached back and showed me the way. Pending is no longer a part of my life nor my speech because I am not undecided about any choices I've made, especially when it comes to serving God and His people for the rest of my life. This is deemed as taking inventory and making wise decisions. Food for thought: Make your own decisions and leave no pending status because the plan and purpose God has for your life may not be the same road map He gave me. Therefore seek Him and choose Him . . . make it quick.

Opinion, everybody has one just respect it

We live in a world where everybody has an opinion. Opinion is defined as a belief or judgment that rest on grounds insufficient to produce certainty. In my terms, opinion is defined as just another person's thoughts about a specific matter in topic of conversation that holds no weight. In this society we all voice our thoughts about subject matters that are mentioned in a discussion or even across the news feed. I do believe in respecting another person's thoughts on a particular subject matter even if I am the topic of conversation. I do not see any reason to get bent out of shape, upset, or react to a person's thoughts. They have a right, as well as you and I, to exercise their freedom of speech. Respect it! If you are confident about who you are and Whose you are then let it roll off your shoulders. We all say that we are mature in every area of our lives . . . somehow this is not always true. Why take a person's opinion of you or a specific subject and allow it to rent space in your head? Don't have a mental head-on collision with their thought process. Step back, look at your life, where you are currently, your accomplishments, the goals God has allowed you to reach, focus and master the definition of an opinion, display confidence, and respect where you are standing. Their thought process remains insufficient to produce certainty, especially if it is about you. Just keep pushing and accomplishing what needs to be accomplished with the smell of victory in your nostrils. This is food for thought: Live stress-free. It's just an opinion and everybody has one, even a child.

If I offended you, tell me!

Oftentimes I wonder if it is cool or even correct to say "if I offended you then tell me". See, we as a people and a race walk around with chips on our shoulders, malice in our hearts, and no road leading to forgiveness. I am not excluding myself from anything because I have been there, done that, and God is still working on me. I am allowing Him to do so strongly in that area. Maybe someone disagreed with your opinion and decision-making. It is not for us to tell that person how they should feel. We are not them, nor are we walking in their shoes to tell them how they should feel. If an individual states that they are hurt by our actions and/or our decisions, keep in mind this is on their side of the tracks with them driving the train. Now, if we care about this person and want to do the right thing - then let us talk about it with them, explain where we were coming from, apologize if we hurt their feelings, and move on. However, if the decision was fair then the one hurting will have to check themselves to see if they are in sensitive mode. Now, when the shoe is on the other foot we can also become a prisoner of our sensitivities. I serve everyone notice including myself that if we find room in our hearts to forgive, forget, maybe even agree to disagree, and move on then the ride will be a lot smoother as well as the landing. This is food for thought: If I offended you then tell me, I can take it. I am grown.

Are you starving?

Some people are in a position where they are starving and some are not. Some are starving to fit in, some are starving to come out from amongst them, some are starving to be successful, and some are starving just to be starving because they cannot determine which way is up. For those of you who are starving to fit in, you must check yourself in a hurry. If you have no insecurities as you say, then people need to fit in with you. Those who are starving to come out from amongst them and cannot, you must check yourself. If you cannot stand to be alone then something is definitely wrong. And for those who are starving to be successful and you have not surrendered it all to God, then problem identified. We must realize and take heed that we need God in all we do. He defines success and without Him you will never reach it. If you are starving just to be starving - - then if a duck can pull a truck then hook him up. We must get out of our own way and allow God to be the driver because He knows the route and has the answers to all of the rocky roads in our lives. When He drive we are definitely accident free instead of accident prone. We as a people must pick up the broken pieces of our lives and turn them over to God. This is food for thought: Starve no more, God has all of the answers to all of our problems.

One of those days

Everyday will not always be Sunday or even sunny. We can look outside the window called life and know what experiences we have allowed to change us for the better and then take a turn for the worse. Example everything appears to be going fine on our side of the road. We wake up one morning and it appears that everything is in mental chaos due to our change of pattern, such as forgetting to pray, fast, trust, and believe. Now, when those things get out of order and we do not do them on a consistent basis then we leave ourselves wide open for chaos. Okay, someone passed by you and said "how are you doing" and you go crazy on them instead of saying "it is one of those days". I guarantee you, that if you place things back in perspective and be consistent with praying, fasting, trusting, and believing chaos will behave and go back to its rightful place. Now, God can make death behave and I do believe that if we stay spiritually organized by praying, fasting, trusting and believing then chaos has no choice but to behave and then IT will say "just one of those days". This is food for thought: Chaos has been removed from my life and it is behaving in compliance with the authority God gave me to speak such a thing.

You overlooked me on purpose

You overlooked me on purpose AND you are saved! I am going to give you a pass on that one. My question is, have you ever been amongst a group of people and someone comes up and starts speaking to everyone in the group but you? Yes, you know that for whatever the reason is this person does not feel you, but they confess to be saved. If this happens we must remain Christ-like, ignore the ignorance, ignore the stupidity, and do not question them. Raise the bar and tell them "God is good, isn't He" and allow the Holy Spirit to convict them. However, you came across to the entire crowd by your actions, as a winner of all winners and most of all Christ-like. If we are saved we do not have to confess it. It will show in our lifestyle that something about us is different. This is food for thought: Check your walk . . . it must line up with your talk. If you confess to be saved, "hello" should include everyone and not exclude anyone and for those of you who think otherwise I give you a pass, because in that moment you knew no better.

They are your children correct?

At times I sit and wonder what runs through the minds and hearts of individuals who have children at an early age. We must practice safe sex if we are not ready for children. It only takes one time. I would like to utilize this scenario where a parent wants to attend an event and someone agreed to keep the children. You must realize that when the event is over it is your responsibility to relieve the sitter in a timely manner. If you are running late then you should place a call to the sitter explaining the situation. If you do not, then this displays no respect for that person nor do you have respect for your children as well as your freedom. I can laugh out loud because I have seen people become angry when the babysitter calls them because they are late and/or have not called. I must stop you dead in your tracks . . . you have no reason to be mad. Keeping your children was a huge favor of the sitter . . . so get home and be respectful towards the babysitter when you get there. Reality check: These are your children, correct? This is food for thought: Clean up the attitude! Because there will be another event and you will need a babysitter for the same children. Therefore, comply with the babysitting regulations and be on time.

The nerve of you

Life and the things in life can take a toll on you if you allow it. My motto is, "to always get the best of life rather than letting it get the best of me". Have you ever been in position where you had to make a decision to kill or be killed spiritually? I know kill or be killed sounds a little bit weird/harsh in being used as encouragement, but I am going to take it there. You are out minding your own business and someone walks up to you that you are very familiar with and says "Oh, you think you are better than us because you received a new position" or "You think you are all that because you have a new high performance vehicle". My people, this is only to name some of the verbal negativity that can place you in a position to kill or be killed spiritually. You know for yourself that everything that has happened in your life to advance you is all because of God and the hard work that paid off. This is how I would have responded . . . "the nerve of you to come up to me, invite yourself into my world, attempt to verbally abuse me, and transfer your spirit of negativity into my moment. I cast it down and send it back to its rightful place and that is hell. How dare you, when God has given us all the same opportunity to love, serve, trust, and believe in Him for all we want, as well as need." Now, it will be the nerve of me to serve you notice that I will not allow you and the spirits who sent you to throw me off course. This ship will dock at success where God is the captain and I am His servant. Therefore, this is the moment where I will make a very wise decision to kill or be killed spiritually. I am not having it and with the good Lord as my witness I will separate and come out from among you. Yes, allow that to take a toll on you. Food for thought: Reevaluate your life and then hopefully you will come on over to the Lord's side where peace resides and other people's opinions or judgment does not matter. Yes, take that along with the verbal black eye you received for being out of order on the approach. My spiritual man still remains intact.

The problem is with you

On the job or even in the corporate world, have you ever experienced rebelliousness from someone you just begin working with and they do not know you? I have and what a mess this can be. It displays that individuals of this caliber does not have a mind of their own. I had two people throughout my working career where I attempted to provide instructions to them about a particular subject matter . . . then out comes this rebellious spirit. I asked if there was a problem with the instructions provided or if there was a problem concerning something that I may have said? The individual never responded. So I asked the Lord, "what is it that I may have done to this individual"? The Lord did not provide me with an answer in the still voice He usually answers in. He gave me a visual and took my mind back a few days before where I saw the individual speaking with another staff member who informed me that this individual did not care for me. All of a sudden it clicked that this person has been fed something negative about me and they do not have sense enough to test my character by observing me while working together . . . shame on them. I held my head up high, did not allow that to break my spirit, break my confidence or even make me think twice. It had already been confirmed. I told the Lord "thank you and to forgive them for they know now what they do or say." Now, taking it a step further I left it alone and continued to be professional and treat that individual with great respect as we continued to work together. At the end of the training period the individual was convicted and asked to treat me to lunch. I was hesitant but I said yes and moved forward. The individual apologized for the way they treated me and expressed that I was nothing like they were told. I responded by saying this is a learning lesson for both of us. Your lesson is to get to know someone for yourself and not allow another to paint a picture of a person or give you guidance on how you should treat the other person. Because the same person that others are trying to detour you from could very well be the same person God uses to bless you. My lesson learned is to keep doing what I am doing, working on forgiving, working on forgetting, working on allowing the Holy Spirit to lead as well as guide me, and continue to be about my Father's business that I can see clearer and overlook the small things. Therefore, the problem is not with me but with your rebellious soul. This is food for thought: Leave the judgment to God. Step back and take your hands off.

Life is a situation

Well, after sitting and having some alone time a question came across my mind asking "if I can really call life a situation". However, after looking back over my life and knowing that a situation is defined as a location or position with reference to an environment; this made me think about how God allowed separation to come between me and some friends because I did not heed His warning of knowing when to separate and give Him my undivided attention. When you and a person, place or thing are inseparable then God is overlooked. The separation came and we ended up parting ways on a bad note. We have not spoken nor attended specific events if we knew the other would be present. In passing, when we see each other we do speak but keep it moving, as the street terminology defines it. Now, I thank God for the separation and hope that the other friends do also. Had it not been for the separation, God would have been overlooked. The separation allowed me to go through some changes, seek God more, come full circle with the plan and purpose He has for my life, and allowed my discernment to be fined tuned placing me in an arena of people who love and respect me, people who reached their hand out and said come and follow me, and people who love the Lord as much as I do. See everything that appears bad or feel bad is not always so. It works out for your good, allowing room for growth and development. God, I say thank you for many separations. Life is a situation . . . I am in a new location with You, I am positioned, and my environment is no longer polluted. This is food for thought: Life is a situation and I am a part of it.

Calling it like I see it

It is so funny how time flies when you are having fun. If we are going to be atmosphere changers and problem solvers it can only be done by supporting truth and living it as well. You must call it like you see it. If you see someone doing wrong and they ask you for your input it should always be truth. I had someone that was a dear friend of mine who cheated on his wife constantly. That came to an end when they were struck with terminal illness. My friend informed me that he had asked his wife for forgiveness for all that he had done and took her through unnecessarily. The conversation went on and the moment came when he asked "did I do the right thing concerning my wife?" I replied, "how does it feel in your spirit? Are you okay with it?" He replied, "yes I am." During the conversation I told him that he should have asked God for forgiveness first and then ask his wife for it. I also told him that his wife must do the same by asking God for forgiveness and then she must ask his ex-wife for forgiveness, because she interrupted his marriage to her. I explained that the reason he cheated on his wife was because he made that his nature and that his wife is experiencing the same thing but on a harsher level for what she took the ex-wife through. Additionally, I explained that If they were concerned about doing things correctly to clear the slate then the ex-wife is due an apology also. The current wife must realize that she was a participant in violating God's law as it relates to marriage and if she has never apologized for the role she played, then she must do it and do it with urgency. I am saying urgency because we must all urgently seek repentance/forgiveness daily because we do not know when our time may expire. I am calling it like I see it, hate it or love it. I am speaking truth and nothing but the truth. This is food for thought: Get it ALL right not just some of it.

The power of prayer and following God's instructions

I know at times life and people can do things to totally take our attitude in a different direction. For instance, say you are in a place mentally, you have commanded your morning according to scripture, and you spent time with the Lord prior to work. All is well and dandy while you are driving to work, but as soon as you get there something jumps off and the devil makes you feel that commanding your morning has not worked. However, you stick to it by declaring and decreeing such a thing and asking God for forgiveness if you have gone out of your element. We will continue to pray about it and allow the Lord to do just what He said He would do and that is make the enemy your footstool. Yes, just recently I was in a similar situation where I apologized to an individual for their rudeness to me. I know I have to pray for my enemies and ask God to allow His word to sustain me and refrain me from going over the edge on someone who is not worth the time of day. Well, a week and a half after the incident the individual came back and apologized to me. Being a child of the King I had no choice but to accept it and continue to move on. This is food for thought: Do not allow anyone to rent space in your head . . . just tell them "no room, no vacancies, I am all filled up."

I had someone stop me in the hallway today

I wonder, have you ever been at work and allowed your mind to stay on Jesus all day? Throughout the work day you read your declarations, you decree and declare, walk on the outside of the building praying and talking to God, and allow the sweet sounds of the spirituals to grace your ears. By afternoon break you run into a co-worker in the hallway, and they try to strike up a conversation with you while you're on your way to the restroom . . .here comes the devil attempting to have you act like him or out of your Christian character by saying what he wants. I did this and had to check myself. This very well could have been a divine opportunity to encourage, empower, and most of all minister to a soul that may not know how to turn it over to Jesus. Well, when I exited the restroom the coworker asked a question relating to work place drama with a supervisor. I listened very carefully. They wanted to know if I had ever used vacation time in the place of sick time. I explained it all depends on your supervisor, but the standard rule and regulation states that if you are out sick and have exhausted all of your sick time and there's vacation time available then you can use that. The coworker explained that they had attended a meeting and on the way out of the meeting they advised the supervisor that they would be taking sick the remainder of the day. The supervisor responded that this could not be done. I informed the individual that according to the regulations the supervisor is right. The coworker mentioned that their last boss used to allow it. I informed the individual that I witnessed the same situation and I had a past supervisor who allowed that. But with the changing of the guard policies and procedures must be followed. Therefore, make the adjustment, meet the standard of the regulation, and let not your heart be troubled. We must do what is right. This is food for thought: Doing what is right should never be a problem! If it is, then search yourself, take inventory, and with the Spirit of conviction being activated ensure that you do the right thing and be at peace.

The return

In my lifetime people have always said that life is just like history, it repeats itself. Return is defined as to go or come back, as to a former place, position, or state. In life we put out negative things about people we don't like, we put out positive things about people we love, and in general we put something out just to be doing something. Life is like a computer, whatever you put in is what you will get out in return. There goes that word return again . . . it will return back where it came from in full return. If I plant bananas I cannot expect to sprout oranges, it will not happen like that. We must be careful of what we allow to enter our ear gates and what exits out of our mouth gates. Whatever happened to do unto others as you will have them do unto you? I serve you notice that lip service is a serious business that can make or break someone. Some things are hard to recover from. This walk in life is not easy. Each time we ask for forgiveness for something we have done it should make us cautious in thinking before we speak and to become wiser and not dumber in attempting to ruin someone else. This is definitely food for thought: Whatever is on your mind think about it before you open your mouth and speak it or send it out into the universe. Once it is out there the damage is done.

Give support then you will receive support

We all know that in life we have hosted events, attended events, and/or promoted events. When you begin to promote and send out invitations you knew who would attend, who would not attend, and who will make an excuse for not coming even though they knew they weren't coming anyway. I was always taught that when you give support you receive support in return. Sometimes it breaks our heart when the ones we always support never come out and give support in return. All I can say is laugh out loud and hold your head up high because whoever was in attendance is who God wanted there in the first place. It is not about us but about God and what He will use to encourage another. We have been taught that we do not do evil for evil - vengeance is the Lord's. I do believe that if you are always looking for and expecting the support of others but never return the favor, God will allow that support to go elsewhere . . . and you can't blame anyone but yourself. You reap what you sow. You see, nothing from nothing leaves nothing and you must give something if you want to be around me. This is food for thought: Learn to give support then you will never have to worry about a shortage, because sometimes people are just blessed by your presence.

I am just wondering

Have you ever been sitting and just having a quiet moment meditating on the Lord and His doings? It has happened to me and while sitting here I received a "check-up" call from a friend of mine. I started telling her about my weekend and about the life of my aunt who we had just buried. I proceeded to tell her that I was flying to Atlanta the coming Thursday and she stated that she only take the train when she traveled. I laughed and said that while everyone else on the plane was on their computers, listening to music, reading magazines, and/or conversing with each other, I'll be reading the word of God and praying for safe travel. So if the plane happened to run into trouble and if it goes down, I'll still be standing - clutching the Word. Because as the saying goes, "everything is going down but the Word of God". She laughed until she couldn't stop and said that was a good one. This is food for thought: If you believe in God and His word like that, then you will survive and rise above the occasion at all times. I believe! His word will not return void.

Coming in the nick of time

Have you ever asked the Lord for something and it appears He has not heard you or even answered? Because we want it in our timing. I have something that I prayed and rejoiced unto the Lord for and when it came I could hardly gain my composure. I was laid off from September 2012 to September 2013 . . . an entire year. I thought it was rough but the Lord showed me that He was in the midst and controlling things the whole time. After returning to the work force, the same department where people said negative things about me were placed on layoff status . . . the ENTIRE department. Now, they are all faced with the same thing I was faced with. I remember that day so clearly when I walked out, I said to the people "do not worry about me because Whom I serve will take very good care of me. When I receive my next job you all will be losing yours." The layoff was unethical and maybe even what I said at the time might have been as well. However, I prayed, asked God for forgiveness, and asked God to deliver the people and make a way so that not a one will be without a job or have a delay in income. Yes, this was my prayer even for the ones who said it was good I got laid off. That statement was made because they personally did not like the truth I stood for nor could they deal with the confidence I had in the God I served. The day came where one hundred and seventy-seven people were being laid off as of June 30, 2014 and the Lord answered my prayer for them. God delivered! Here is what He did - of the one hundred and seventy-seven layoffs, one hundred and seventy received job offers. In addition, three people from another department retired around this same time which left three positions vacant to be filled by the layoffs. Now, however God decides to work this thing out is all on Him. People of God this is something to rejoice and praise Him for because He knew what was up ahead. I am calling it like I see the miracle that was performed by the only wise God. Some can say He comes in the nick of time, but for me and my house He is always on time. You better praise Him while you still have the chance. This is food for thought: Do not credit man, but credit God for using man concerning us. Now take that to the bank, cash it and deposit it.

When a woman loves

It is so funny how we go through life as a boy and then a man. The growth is so amazing to see, especially when we experience love on a level where it can cause us to be a bit afraid of getting hurt. A woman places her all into love on a level to where I think we as men may be afraid to take it at some point. When a woman loves she shares with her female friends, speak with her mother about it, speak with her pastor about it, and if need be speak with the partner who may have caused her hurt. We as men when love hurts us we are afraid to share with our homeboys and we play tough on the exterior knowing that the interior is on the verge of being destroyed because of love. Because of the pain we end up talking under a woman's clothes which is so disrespectful and less of a man, and because of the pain we will try and go through it alone. As for me, I am not afraid to go after a woman if I love her. If she hurts me, if I did something to turn her away, and even if she decides that someone else has caught her eye I am more than willing to give it one more try before we decide to throw it all away. If we men can get to this point then the respect we long for will be willingly displayed by the woman we love. Yes, it will transform to an entirely different level to where a woman will say this man loves me and I will do right by him. I do not see a problem with being "soft" for love. Even though we may not admit it, we've all been there at least once in our lives. Say what you want to say, I am going to call it like I see it and that is when a woman loves she loves for real. This is food for thought: Do not allow the real experience or the one you know you love get away. However, if she decides to let go because she thinks the grass is greener on the other side at least you can say "I tried". The bird that flies away is not ours unless it fly back on its on. This means I tried, she denied me and now I am moving on because me, life, time, and God will not wait forever.

The Barber Shop

Wow, how funny it is to listen to men in a barber shop talk about specific issues. I was receiving a service in the barber shop the other day and a conversation came up about black and white relationships. In comes a customer and he took a seat in the barber's chair and said he was having a great day. The customer mentioned that neither his daughter nor son could bring home someone of Caucasian descent. Someone asked why and he said because he did not like people of that ethnic background. I placed myself in the conversation and said that I respect your choice for you and your house, but love does not have a color. Then an employee at the shop said "well I have three baby mothers and one of them is white . When we were together we had fun and enjoyed each other and up until this day we are still cordial to one another but can't be in a relationship because it did not work." Later a friend of the barbers enters and said he feels that Caucasian women treated black men better and they do not give back-talk. A female barber indicated that she did not agree with that. She stated that if some black men knew how to treat a black woman and be fair to her, showing respect, then she would respond better. The friend of the barbers stated that he'd rather be with a woman of the Caucasian descent but do not want his children to be in a relationship with any of them. The female barber then stated that if she choose to date a man of Caucasian descent then it is her choice. She felt she would have no problem dealing with him because he couldn't treat her any worse than the men of black descent. So color does not matter. I said it all depends on the mindset of both individuals in that relationship. Many were raised to see color as a factor. A product of their environment. It was mentioned by someone entering the barber shop, catching the tail-end of the conversation, that we all have poor mindsets based on what our mothers and fathers went through. I said I did not agree and that it did not apply to me. Simply because I was not assigned to what my mother and father experienced as far as it relates to segregation and what they went through. Yes, I've heard the horror stories told by my parents and others who were a part of that era. But I will not allow it to stagnate me or even hold me back from where I am headed today. Again, that was not assigned to me and that was not my experience. Therefore, my mindset is different, that segregation assignment was not assigned to me, and I am living in a different era where it is handled as well as tolerated differently. I am one individual, one human, and one man so you must speak for yourself. I am not poor but rich because the word of God tells me that the power of life and death lies in the tongue and whatever I request of my Father it shall be granted. I am looking good right now but even better in my future. This is food for thought: Live and talk about your own experience and not become stagnated by living someone else's story. Transform your mind and allow the Lord to provide direction which is the way of escape and I will not accept anything outside of that. I don't think so!

Straight with no cut on it

I am going to put it to you straight with no cut on it. Things have happened to each of us in life. However, it is up to us to decide if we will live from it, die from it, learn from it, advance from it, and/or leave it in the past where it belongs. Yes, you will have people who will not always agree with you, not always like you, not always be in your corner, not always see the vision God has for you, and some who will just be who they are. However, I will not worry about any of that because when God gave me the green light to move forward I took advantage of that divine opportunity. He controls my destiny and the end-results, not the people who have all of these hang-ups. I have experienced hurt and disappointment but when I learned that my trust should always be in the only wise God then I know I will always overcome what may come my way. People like to use the word struggle, but that does not work for me because the Holy Bible tells me that I will overcome and that I am more than a conqueror and more than a conqueror I am. I will not give negativity the power to tell me how high I can jump, how low I can duck, if I can reach for the stars, if the sky is the limit for me, or even how far I can go in life. If you look in my eyes and see what I see then you will know that what you say, how you judge, and how you see me and my accomplishments has absolutely no impact on me at all. While you are placing so much energy into what you think I should be doing and where I should be going, guess what? I am already there. You are a day late and a dollar short. This is food for thought: I am giving it to you straight with no cut on it. You can only see where you are and what you have experienced. Yes, I have moved on a long time ago. You are talking instead of walking by placing judgment on something you have no authority to do so.

How did I make it over

Changes, changes, changes, and more changes! Sometimes things happen that causes us to become angry with people and life in general. However, we must pray to God and ask Him to assist us in making adjustments in meeting this newfound change that has impacted our being. Keep in mind that God always knows what is up ahead. He is the only One who can make the load a little lighter and give us the strength to carry on when we are about to throw in the towel and call it quits. We cannot win if we quit nor will we know what victory feels like if we give in. Now, I can name a few changes that have impacted my life and some that I saw impact the lives of others; such as medical conditions that were very life threatening, bad car accidents, homelessness, mental health issues, disabilities, etc. However, we can look at these issues/changes and still give God the glory. It was He who gave us this extended stay on this place called earth. I feel like shouting, I feel like clapping my hands, I feel like saying Hallelujah, and I feel like thanking God for being so good to me. This is food for thought: My soul looks back and wonder how I made it over.

Garbage in the church

We all know that the church is supposed to be our safe haven. A place where we can go and have our spirits lifted, where you can feel the purity with your hands, and a place where the Most High and His mandates are followed through at all times. I have news for you because times has changed and even people in the church have changed. I want to once again give it to you straight by stating the facts. In churches these days you see people walk past you and not speak; women wearing clothing too tight, splits up the caboose, entire back out, dresses and skirts so short that if they coughed it would fly over their heads; bickering; back biting; hearsay; fighting; and prostitution of the gospel just to get ahead. On the streets prostitution is the oldest trick in the book and God does not need a pimp for His word. However, I know some may not have all the necessary things needed to be dressed appropriately. But with these individuals you can tell - - because a lot of other areas are lacking as well due to temporary circumstances beyond their control. If you have to continuously pull your dress or skirt down you knew it was too short before you left home. Now, men that goes for us as well. Do not come to church just to find a woman, displaying your gold teeth, the whips on your ride, confronting another man about making passes at your girl, wearing your pants so tight until it is a distraction to the service, and even talking loud on your cell with the ringer turned all the way up. Yes, we all have faults. What has happened to the respect that we owe God the Father first, the church second, the leaders in the church third, and the remainder of the body? See, garbage is defined as a place or receptacle where rubbish is discarded or a worthless, useless, or unwanted matter. Now a days it's hard to tell the church from the streets and the people of God from the people of the world. God does not need us nor our garbage. It is unwanted. We must do that which is right and not settle for that which is wrong. Let us show God and His house respect as well as those He has placed in leadership. Leaders, we are to display the same in return. Because we are not exempt from God's law. This is food for thought: Our garbage is unwanted by the Man in charge - - which is God. Remember, church is not the streets and the people of God should not be people of the world. Christianity is a lifestyle and so is the lifestyle of the world. Now ask yourself which one are you living and displaying. I am not talking condemnation, just stating the facts of what has been witnessed with my own two eyes. I had to also take an inventory of myself and re-stock with better products.

Taking correction in the church

Yes, correction can be hard at times especially when we have one foot in the church, the other in the world, and we're unwilling to surrender totally. I am a living witness to where correction has made me upset, dislike the one who rendered correction, unwilling to give up a lifestyle which was pleasing to me, enjoyed doing wrong, and just wanting to be about what I thought was my business and not God's. Oh man what a mess, to confess to have changed for the better but unable to take correction in the church. Trials come to test our faith. But the test should cause us to develop and get past the small things such as thinking our way is always right, having a one track mind when it comes to correction, having tunnel vision when it comes to correction, believing it's our way or the highway, and thinking that you don't have to submit to anything because you're "grown". Laugh out loud! Because once upon of time I thought and felt the same way. I was "so called" grown but still throwing temper tantrums like a child. A true sign of immaturity. In the church today we show no love and commitment to one another which divides a house, church, and ourselves. With this type of attitude we cannot stand. The word of God tells us a house divided cannot stand. Why can't we handle correction in the church when we handled it in the world? When we decide to live for God we should become stronger and not weaker, we become wiser, more respectful, accept correction quicker than anyone else, do not become offended about every little thing, and we love easily. The question still remains, what happened to handling correction in the church? Well, I can no longer question it nor question the behavior of others. However, I just have to ensure that I am on the right track and take my correction like a man . . . an adult. All I can say is we better get it right! It is not the huge things that always break up a relationship but the small things, which have a stronger impact and causes more division. My relationship with God means a lot to me. This is food for thought: Whatever happened to handling correction in the church? Lord, please tell me.

Give from the saucer and not the cup

We all can say that once upon a time we gave our all to life and to the people in our lives. At times we gave so much until we forgot about ourselves, placing others first. We have all heard that it is better to give than to receive. To me that is correct to a certain extent. If God the Father continuously give us the blessings that we request in order to make our lives better then how will we enjoy it when we keep giving it all away. I do believe that some blessings are to be enjoyed rather than given away. Example, we have given time to people, love to people, money to people, hugs to people, kisses to people, respect to people, honor to people, and even our last to people. However, when it is our turn to be in need we can't even get a hello, good-bye, a handshake or even some of the same things in return. I am not saying help a person just to see if they can help you in return, but at least be considerate when I am in need rather than ignore me. Now that I am wiser and still have a heart for people I will have one for myself. I understand now that when the Lord blesses me to share it's not from what he placed in my cup but to share from what is on the saucer. The cup symbolizes what He has given to me for my labor of standing firm on His word and the help I have rendered to others because He instructed me to or caused me to discern that they were in need and at the time I was able to supply it. The saucer is for those who are always in need, never a blessing to others, or will never give to others even though they have it. Yes, give from the saucer which symbolizes the residue. Residue is defined as a small amount of that which remains after something has been removed or completed. This is food for thought: I know you get my drift that God intended for all of us to have. But I cannot continue to give you the fruits of my labor when you refuse to labor for your own.

Me, God, and the outside vendor

Have you ever been in conversation with the Lord and here comes a phone call, a knock at the door, or some other distraction? When we begin to get in a place with God, the devil sees it. He sends his distractions any way possible to detour us from spending time with the Lord and doing His work. Example, on the job, to serve all clients sometimes a contract or an agreement is established with an agency to provide unoffered services to those clients. This is to prevent a delay in rendering services to those in need or cause a delay in the company functioning. In life we have outside vendors as it relates to relationships, bills, living arrangements, conversations, car accidents, upsets that make us leave the church, etc. WE must allow God to speak to our spirit and provide guidance on how to handle the outside vendor. To me an outside vendor can be defined in many ways, such as a distraction, interruption, interference, the uninvited, and so on. The devil is also an outside vendor who invites himself into things and our lives where he is unwanted. However, he can definitely come when we are not doing what we are supposed to do as Christians such as praying, meeting the mandates of God's law, breaking the mandate of the law created by man to govern the state, agreeing with the wrong when we know it is not right, and when we are in a position to rightfully divide the word of truth and we don't based on favoritism these things can and has caused us to err. I can say when we know better we are responsible for doing better on every level of the law created by God according to his manual "The Bible". I will not allow the outside vendor to interrupt my covenant with the Lord. I am following His direction concerning my walk and will not allow one of the outside vendors known as "man" to make any adjustments to it by preaching, teaching, and ministering his own doctrine instead of the word developed by God. This is food for thought: I have cancelled my contract with the outside vendor and the distractions that come along with it, and I am not changing my mind. Therefore, watch out for the outside vendor because most of the services they offer are not always good. So be gone!

The true meaning of confidentiality

We all have someone in our life that we feel has been placed there to share things with, talk about specific situations, share our upcoming thoughts, and one who we can talk to and never have to tell them don't say anything - - this conversation is between us. We should all understand that confidentiality means to be in strict privacy, secrecy, or imparting a private matter. Have you ever shared something with a close friend whom you felt would never expose/reveal something you all talked about in confidentiality? But one day it was brought to your attention that it was revealed. It makes you feel violated and that you should have never shared it. Trust is out the window. You become angry over their actions, separating you from them. I am here to tell you that when you feel violated, sometimes it is to the point of no return. It places the respect and friendship on another level where shorter visits and phone calls come into play. Well, I will keep it real or one hundred as the street terminology defines it. If I cannot trust you, cannot share the simple things with you, have to guide you on what to repeat and what not to repeat, and if I have to say it is strictly between us, then our friendship needs to be re-evaluated and sent to the oral review board with me as chief in command. Now check this, I am not mad with you . . . but I will never share anything else with you; I am not mad with you . . . but the respect has been lost; I am not mad with you . . . but we have no trust as friends; I am not mad with you . . . but I will respectfully feed you with a long handled spoon; and I am not mad with you . . . but you caused this re-evaluation not me, so blame yourself. Because your loose lips sank the ship and I am no longer in need of a personal assistant. This is food for thought: Confidentiality and friends do not mix, but God and confidentiality does. I am not mad at you, but you need to be alone and figure yourself out.

I wonder

We've all did and said something that made you question where it came from. Yes, we've experienced mood swings and attitude problems, with no consideration of others, their time, and their patience. I wonder . . .

what if God didn't love us,
what if God saw us as the scum of the earth,
what if God had zero tolerance for our foolishness,
what if God did not give us chance after chance,
what if God said He don't fool with us,
what if God threw up in our face every time we asked Him for help,
what if God shamefully talked bad about us,
what if God kicked us when we were down,
I wonder, I wonder, I wonder, and I wonder.

Well, we should give Him total praise and take a look back over our lives to see just how far the Lord has brought us. Even when we had no regard for Him He still blessed us. See, if God was like us the world and its people would be in worse shape than they are right now and we would really have to wonder. We should just give Him glory non-stop with "thank You, Jesus" continuously flowing from our lips. This is food for thought: If we always did what was right concerning God, His grace, and His people we would not have to wonder "what if". Because His grace and mercy follows us all the days of our lives.

Keep some things separate

We all know someone that can "get it cracking", "popping", disturb the peace, and some who are just quiet. My mother always told me that if I would learn to hear and don't hear, see and don't see, keep and don't keep, inhale and exhale then I would be able to handle things a lot better. I do believe that I can learn more by being quiet and observing those around me. For instance, say you may see me getting my praise on in church, helping around the church, talking with my brothers and sisters in Christ, and/or even encouraging some in church, but see me on the streets and we may just only speak to each other in passing. This does not mean that we are not cordial or that we only respect each other in church. I do believe in keeping some things separate . . . not mixing church associates with work associates, mixing work associates with personal associates or even mixing personal associates with business associates. A lot of times the groups do not mix well and there is no need for anyone to get it twisted or try forcing it. Business and friendship definitely don't mix and I know how to separate the two. For instance, when it comes to business my friends must take a backseat because business is a priority in its own arena and in that order. This is food for thought: Just like that! Keep some things and some people separate because they are like oil and water, they do not mix.

I am so check it

Sometimes, I like to begin with a question to my supporters. Have you ever thought about who you are and Whose you are? I am sure you have. If you had parents that loved and validated you at home you had no need to be validated by looking for love all in the wrong places. I have no problem with telling people who I am, Whose I am, and what characteristics I possess that makes me all that I am. With Christ and in Christ I am ALL THAT and some. I am more than a conqueror, I am blessed, I am chosen, I am accepted, I am redeemed through His blood, I am marvelous, I am great, I am above, I am first, I am strong, I am a miracle, I am favor, I am faith, I am responsible, I am in authority, I am ahead, I am stable, I am rich and I do mean rich, I am God's anointed, I am God's appointed, I am a servant, I am a king, I am wonderfully made, I am powerful, and I AM all of that and more. Don't believe it? Then check the word of God. It has been declared as well as decreed and it gets no better than this. Laugh out loud . . . I know you are saying that I am not all of that, that is your opinion. Because greater is he that is in me than he that is in the world. This is not arrogance but confidence in the only wise God. He did not make junk or mistakes in creating me. I walk boldly in Him. This is food for thought: In Christ I am all of that and more because my confidence and security is in Him and no one else. Therefore, I am great and great I am.

No Chaser

Well, when you tell someone that you are going to tell it like it is this means to me that you are giving it to them straight like a drink with no chaser. I have had different scenarios where I had to inform someone that I had zero tolerance for things that are downright foolish and of no relevance to me. For example, I was having a conversation with someone who said they were so in love with their child while denying having any feelings for the other parent. During the conversation I asked, "why is it that when you are angry with the other parent you stop dealing with the child you claim you love? Why is it that when you can't control the other parent, you stop dealing with the child you claim you love? Why is it that when the other parent wouldn't accept your foolish way of living, you stop dealing with the child you claim you love?" I stated that that isn't love because if you did then the child would always be priority whether you and the other parent are together or not. The child should not have to witness or be a part of the immaturity of adults. The child must be respected and not be placed in a position to choose sides causing the child emotional dysfunctional. Both parents need to check themselves, grow up, take control of your behavior, act as responsible adults, place things in perspective, communicate exceptionally well on behalf of the child, realize that it is not about you anymore now that a child is involved and accept the fact that the relationship is over. String up your shoes, move forward, and save the child. This is food for thought: I gave it to you straight with no chaser, no coke, or orange juice, but the truth. God loves the truth. It may make us mad but it will definitely straighten us out. Accept it or deny it, because truth is what it is and does what it does.

The facts of a verdict

We as people believe in waiting to see what the final verdict is without even being in court. I always laugh because the verdict could very well be whatever the gossip is and not the gospel. Verdict is clearly defined as the decision made by a jury in a trial or even a judgment or opinion about something. For instance, when a person loses a lot of weight, without even knowing the reason, people start gossiping. Many come up with their own diagnosis that they associate with weight loss, such as AIDS. It is so funny how people can take something and run with it, damaging reputations because of hearsay. Yes, they render a verdict without any supporting evidence. So what if someone loses weight, skin appears darker than usual, completely lose their appetite, or you see their medication knowing that it is used to treat AIDS. It still does not mean that they have it. I serve you notice that steroids is an anti-inflammatory medication and it is used to treat many illnesses including AIDS. All I am saying is do your homework. If you want to render diagnosis or verdicts then get the degrees to do it. This is food for thought: Don't get caught up in the hype of gossip, it'll make life easier. Strive to do something more productive that will assist in making your creditability dependable and believable. Gossip the Gospel!

A powerful being

In so many ways we can say that we are powerful beings. But it has no merit if you are not confident. Powerful is defined as having the ability to control or influence people or things. In addition, it can also mean having a strong effect on someone or something producing a lot of physical strength. In separating the two being is defined as existence, the nature or essence of a person, a real or imaginary living creature who is especially intelligent. Take a look back over your life, people flock to you, respect you, believe in you, and at some point became a loyal follower or listener as it relates to supporting you. These people should never be taken for granted or misused because they are dependable and play a major role in empowering us in getting to the next destination or level in life. We must see everyone as significant. I was always taught there are no big "I's" and little "U's". The word of God states "we all are servants". Now, I do not want someone that I can control because I will not be controlled, I do not want a "yes" person because I am not a "yes" person, and I do not want someone who is weak - - who will stand for nothing and fall for anything or anyone. I do believe that if two are on one accord they can become a force to be reckoned with. Even if there is only one, and they know who they are, Whose they are, and where they are headed, to me they are a powerful being. It's evident in those who are confident and comfortable in who they have been designed to be. This is food for thought: Be strong without allowing people to make you second guess if you are a powerful being or not. They very well know that you are and this is why they are chasing you down. So grab the opportunity and advance because you are a powerful being and a powerful being you are.

Pieces of me

All this mean is that parts of my life are being used to bless someone . . . in letting them know that we are all human. Pieces is defined as to assemble something from individual parts. See, we can take notice of another person's life, their mistakes, their growth, and their development to build character within ourselves. We all have gone through trials and tribulations but looking at someone else's life can alert us to the warning signs of trouble that we may avoid or overcome. We are empowered by the triumph of others. Encouraged by their victory through prayer and faith. Even as an adult we can learn from the experiences of others. You may have experienced a life changing situation that you can tell someone about by letting them know that change is good. I serve notice that we all have been placed on earth because of the double "P's", which means plan and purpose. Plan is defined as a detailed proposal for doing or achieving something; and purpose is defined as the reason for something being done or created for which something exist. Therefore, this is food for thought: You are a living, detailed proposal placed on this earth to share with others. Remember, you have been spiritually assigned to others by a Higher Power. Therefore, be a good leader instead of a follower . . . you are the head and not the tail.

I blame you!

In this world we all have experienced blame. Blame is defined as to hold responsible or find fault with. At times in our childhood when we were afraid of getting in trouble with our parents for violating the rules set to govern the household. We would shift the blame to other sibling. Cowardly, adults blame others when they don't want to be held accountable for their own shortcomings. As adults it's time to put away childish things, conquer your insecurities and fears, and own up to your own shortcomings and stop placing the blame on others. This is food for thought: Get out of your own way because you are blocking your own blessings with all of this hate-r-ration.

Pleasure principle

Pleasure is something we look for from time to time and it is defined as a feeling of happy satisfaction and enjoyment, used or intended for entertainment, or to give sexual enjoyment and satisfaction. For those involved in a relationship or marriage this is a key element of satisfaction. Principle is defined as a moral rule or belief helping us to know what is right and what is wrong that influences our actions. For those seeking the pleasure principle outside of marriage and commitment, living promiscuously, and placing innocent people in danger, the wages of sin is death. We all have desires, but do not take your body which is identified in the Bible as a temple and use it for self gain or to make a name for yourself. Save yourself! Because when you have sexual relations with another person you transfer spirits with them, maybe becoming even more promiscuous. Calm down, settle down, be faithful to the one you plan on sharing the remainder of your life with and be faithful to yourself and God as well. We must not do anything to befoul the temple that God built and breathed life into. This is food for thought: If you like taking on other spirits in addition to the ones you already have then go ahead. The end result of promiscuousness is death. The graveyard has room for everyone. Just settle down and be wiser.

Take me as I am and I do mean take me as I am

What you see is what you get! I am not making any enhancements to my body to satisfy no one. I am proud of the way God has created me in His own image. Whoever wants to be with me must take me as I am. I can only be me. What about you? Are you on the verge of making enhancements to get a man or woman? Or are you doing it because of health issues? Beauty is in the eye of the beholder, and I am the beholder when it comes to me and I don't think, I know that all is good over here. I am intelligent, I have set standards, and I know love does not have a color or face. To the ladies, the Bible states that "he who finds a wife finds a good thing," not she that finds a husband. Ladies, don't be in a hurry because in due time what is for you God will grant it and it will work in your favor. This is food for thought: It is okay to want a mate to share and spend time with but do not appear to be desperate, settling for something that wasn't ever intended for you. Wait on God! Don't move ahead of Him.

The interaction between Men and Women

Interaction takes place in everyday life. Interaction is defined as talking, looking, sharing, and engaging in any kind of action that involves men and women. However, interaction does not justify or support the act of domestic violence. Things do happen and may not be as crazy or as drastic as it may seem but still we should not result to physical or even mental abuse. Men are not here to beat their women. We are to cherish her, love her, respect her, and treat her like a queen. Women, you have criteria you must meet as well in representing your man, respecting him, encouraging him, and standing by his side. I want to place a check on a few things as it relates to interaction . . . once a boy becomes a man and girl becomes a woman they cannot be raised again. Therefore, we have to stop provoking each other to anger, then the thought of kill or be killed will be erased and we can reason with each other. We must think before we react, still love one another without media or law involvement, and get past what fueled it to begin with. Interacting allows for room to reason and understand each other for the betterment of the union.

Don't just talk . . . . communicate
Don't just look . . . . observe and pay attention
Don't just share . . . . . connect
Don't just engage . . . . love

This is food for thought: Let us all do better towards one another and push toward the mark of supporting each other in this thing called relationship. However, rule out domestic violence with "united we stand divided we fall." Love conquers all.

Relationship between confession and forgiveness

Confession is defined as a written or spoken statement in which you admit to have done something wrong or committed a crime. Forgiveness on the other hand is defined as to stop feeling anger towards someone who has done something wrong, to stop blaming. Have you ever been backed into a corner and had to confess the truth about something you lied about? After owning up to it you realized that it would have been less intimidating and a whole lot easier to tell the truth from the beginning. Once you confess, it makes it easier for those you impacted to forgive. It's the same way with God. We confess and He forgives. My belief is, just like grace and mercy works together so does the relationship between confession and forgiveness. It's a one-way street . . . Confessing to God leads to forgiveness from God. Only He can make the crooked way straight.

Stay in position

Life itself can make you dysfunctional. Have you ever asked yourself, why? Have you searched for answers in all the wrong places? Or did you just give up? We all have been at our lowest and didn't know which way to go or who to turn to in our time of need. When we look back this can be a laugh out loud moment, because we ended up getting out of position, moving from under the cover of safety, and/or not staying the course. One thing about it, God never sleeps nor slumber. He knows everything that is going on. We must stay in position and not move until the Holy Spirit instructs us to. No matter how hard times appear, keep your hands lifted up and your mouth filled with praise. Stay focused and stay the course. Remember, in order to get something we are required to do something . . . pray non-stop. This is food for thought: We are responsible for maintaining our position and staying the course. So don't make it hard, just do it.

The blessing is

Blessing is defined as a special favor, mercy, benefit, liberty, or something contributing to or promoting happiness. On the other hand I will define it as something out of the ordinary or uncommonly done by God that amazes mankind. Example, one day I was at the gas station. I pulled up to the pump, and as I exited the vehicle I felt someone watching me. I turned around and a lady was staring me in the face as if she wanted to say something, but she didn't. I proceeded to go in and pay for the gas. I was standing there wondering why this lady was looking at me so strangely. When I headed back out to pump the gas she said, "excuse me, can I ask you something?" I replied, yes. She said, "I'm in between paychecks and have no gas to make it to my next destination. Can you spare some gas?" I informed her that once I was done pumping gas I would check to see what I had left. The spirit of discernment led me to believe that she was sincere and was indeed in need. So I went back inside the station and paid what I had left on my card. I came back out and let her know how much I was able to give (which unknowing to her was my last). She pumped the gas, turned to me and said, "thank you and God bless you". I said to myself, "God, was this You?" It felt so right. The following day while in the check-out line at the grocery store a young lady behind me said, "I know you from somewhere." I said, "I don't think I really know you, but cool." She then told the cashier, "I'm going to pay for his groceries." She turned to me and said, "I know you from visiting my church from time to time." I said, yes. The blessing is . . . God rewarded my obedience to serve Him by being a blessing to His child in need. Hallelujah, I shout because it was only God who rewards obedience and faithfulness. This is food for thought: Do as the Lord instructs you without questioning Him. Because the blessing is, He rewards obedience as well.

Receiving what you put out.

Now, a lot of us go through life thinking it's okay tell it like it is and all is well. However, when someone tells us like it is we take offense. I think that if you can voice your opinion and feel that however people deal with it is on them. Well, by that same token if someone else voices their opinion then you should be able to deal with it without taking offense. For instance, I had someone who was a part of my circle of friends and she would always voice her opinion, give her feedback, say what she wanted to say, stand by it strongly, and allow it to be what it is. When the ball was in the other court and feedback was given, opinions voiced and they said what they had to say, stood by it strongly, and allowed it to be what it is was the opposing team member wanted to call a violation. As the old and new sayings go . . . if the shoe fits then wear it; if you can't take the heat then get out of the kitchen; if you don't care for grilled food then don't grill and serve it to someone else; if you are tender-headed then don't go natural; if you don't have a license then don't drive; don't place your foot in a size eight if you know your foot is a ten; don't write a check your behind can't cash, if you speak out on a five dollar conversation that is worth ten cents then expect change in return; all aces served on a tennis court are returnable; and the list goes on. I am sure you get my drift. Do not voice your opinion on something if you do not want the feedback in return. The world does not revolve around you. This is food for thought: Be able to handle it if you put it out. Everyone has an opinion and some people are equipped to come back stronger than you. You should be able to receive what you put out there. If you cannot, then get out the game. So be ready!

Normal sense

What if in a normal sense this could be defined as to introduce a suggestion or a proposal for a future event. As we look over our lives, people will not always see what we see nor will we see what they see. God created us in His own image but did not give us all the same thought process or even the ability to always perceive things in the same manner. What if I were president? What if I was the CEO of one of the largest banks in the world? What if I was Secretary of State? Or what if I was just who God intended for me to be? If I decided to be what God intended me to be, would it be enough? I truly believe within myself that if we could just be satisfied in being what God intended us to be and be faithful without complaining everything that we hope, wish, and pray for will be added. This is food for thought: Sit back and watch God add and subtract from your life. If we give Him total control we would not have to ask for anything because when we look back over our lives He made us rich in more ways than just in the form of money. Yes, some people are alive and rich and some died rich. Somehow, we are still standing in wealth because God has provided a way of escape that money could never buy and that is His favor.

The element of recognition

Recognition is defined as an act of recognizing. Some things we do will be recognized and some things won't. That is just the way life goes. If you know you have done your best then pat yourself on the back and thank God. Remember, the story about Jesus and Zaccheaus? Where Jesus looked up and saw him in the tree. Jesus already knew Zaccheaus' history and what he was about. So He called him by name and said come down and haste unto me, which means to come quickly. Jesus could have easily said, "hey you come here". But the element of recognition was when He called him by name and then said come. One can say not only was that an element of recognition but also an element of respect, to be called by your name in spite of what you may have done. If there is anyone who is without sin let them cast the first stone . . . Will there be anyone? I think not. We all have sinned and come short of His glory. This is food for thought: Leave the judgment to God for only He has the authority to judge.

The swell delivery

We all know that when it comes to supporting the truth you stand alone and when you tell the truth it cuts deep to where others will not like you for doing just that . . . sticking with the truth. I was being interviewed for a local magazine and the interviewer asked me, "what do you mean by saying you support truth and you will tell the truth with no cut on it?" I explained that truth is what it is and it needs no defense team. It defends itself. When I say "with no cut" it means that it is straight with no chaser and it will be told with supporting facts and not my opinion. Which makes non-supporters scatter with their chatter. The interviewer understood but asked, "are you willing to make adjustments when supporting truth?" I explained than an adjustment is a small alteration or movement made to achieve a desired fit. Truth always fit, but it becomes very uncomfortable to some. I will make an adjustment if the person tells me that they were offended by the way I said it and their feelings were hurt. The Adjustment is: I am willing to make it by analyzing what was said. My delivery was not to hurt in any type of way. The problem wasn't with the truth but with the tone of delivery. So it remained, but with an adjustment to the tone and it was accepted because truth will not change. In closing, truth was still told, supported, and accepted. We must always stick to the truth and never make adjustments for it to fit to make that which is wrong seem right. We will be held accountable in the eyesight of God. This is food for thought: Do not make adjustments for a free seat in hell and call it like you see it with a swell delivery.

Love Under New Management

When we say that we are in love under new management the key word is management. Management is defined as the process of dealing with or controlling things or people. I like to personally define it with two words - - heavy responsibility. As I was taught it takes two to tango, two to have a conversation, and in reality two to be in love. See, at times drama gets old and a one-sided relationship definitely gets old. When two are in love and decide to go their separate ways it could be because the communication is poor and love does not live there anymore. In all we do we must seek Christ, ask Him for direction, and allow Him to teach us how to endure. As I have said many times love does not have a color, love does not have a face, and love does not eliminate forgiveness which provides you the will power to work through the trials and to move forward. If we open the door and be reminded that it does not matter how old we get or how young we may be there is always room for growth and development. Therefore, if love does begin to mistreat you to the point of no reconciliation then free yourself and ask Christ for guidance. However, if you ask for His direction you are most likely to be in love under new management with your responsibility being to wait on the Lord . . . I said wait on Him. This is food for thought: Experience is the best teacher and it takes someone like us to learn that we are in love under new management.

Analyzing the process before speaking

When you analyze something you separate the idea into parts in order to figure out all the nature and interrelationship of all the parts to consider. Many times we've all said something or responded in a way that was hurtful to others, unintentionally. We all know that once it's been spoken it cannot be retrieved. We must analyze what is being said before responding. We do this by analyzing the tone of the conversation, body language, and history. If I approached someone negatively, I would want them to correct me by saying "I analyzed your approach, researched past conversations with you, listened to your tone, witnessed your body language, and reviewed your history and I feel you need to make some changes when you are interacting with me because I have a zero tolerance for disrespect. I do not engage in unruly behavior towards others, and I ensure that my body language lines up with what I am speaking. So excuse yourself from interacting with me because it is taking a toll on my view of you and the energy you are throwing off, and it is unacceptable to all. In closing, you have just been positively checked. Enough to make you think and take an inventory of your behavior where you will think twice about your approach when engaging in conversation with me. This is food for thought: I analyzed and then went in for the target without causing any disruption or disturbance. However, the person has just been analyzed, checked, and freed from ignorance.

The survivor

The survivor is you, me, the word of God, and His plan and purpose for our lives. A survivor is defined as a person who continues to function or prosper in spite of opposition or setbacks. Opposition is defined as a conflict, resistance, or even a disagreement. This life that we live in brings a lot of things our way. I found out in my life that opposition came quicker because I was not spending more time with God, reading the Word was not a daily priority, and I was slacking in other areas. Even though the enemy came in like a flood the Lord still lifted up a standard against him and deemed me a survivor. Yes, it was conflict but I survived, It was disagreements but I survived, it was disappointments but I survived, discouraged but I survived, problems arose in the work place but I survived, problems in the home but I survived, didn't feel like hearing what was right but I survived, made bad choices and did wrong but I survived, I was disobedient and I still survived. This is food for thought: We can learn from other people's experiences. As long as we trust God, His plan and purpose designed for our lives, and continue to function as well as prosper in spite of the opposition or the setback then we will survive . . . we are more than a conqueror.

Experiencing what's real

Experience is defined as the practical contact with and observation of facts and events. In defining experience it brings me to this place, this moment in my writing . . . How can I tell someone God is a healer if I've never experienced His healing power? How can I tell someone God is a miracle worker if I've never experienced His miracle working power? How can I tell someone that God will make a way out of no way if I've never experienced His way making power? How can I tell someone that "God is" if I don't have a relationship with Him to know His presence and His voice when He is providing guidance for me to prevent self destruction? When you are in a relationship with God you know that He can take the simple (foolish) things to confound the wise. An experience with Him can go as follows . . . Have you ever followed the Holy Spirit when It said to check your bank account and you know your account had a zero balance but because of your obedience to the Holy Spirit the money was present when you checked again? Things of this sort happens because it is a miracle working experience with the way making power of the Almighty. Have you ever met someone who was diagnosed with stage four cancer and the doctors did all they were able to do and the individual was given up to die? But when the doctors entered the room for what they thought was the last time, they saw a great turnaround with no evidence of cancer anywhere . I am here to tell you that this is an experience with the miracle working, healing power of the Almighty. Experiences with God are non-fictional, real events that don't contradict His word. In closing, always speak from a place that is factual, based on a real life supernatural experience with the Almighty God. This is food for thought: Believe in miracles everyday because God will make a way out of no way. He is God, just like that.

Give your life to the Lord

We all know that we cannot continue to live our lives in the shape that we are in. The Potter wants to put us back together so that we may reach the place He has prepared for us. I do understand that our lives are not our own and that we were all bought with a price. He will right all of our wrongs if we allow Him. The devil did not die for us. He lives to kill, steal, and destroy us. His deception makes it appear hard to live for the Lord so that he can have his way. This is food for thought: Giving our lives to the Lord is easy even though we make living for Him hard. Again, the devil paints a clearer picture and draws what appears to be an easier road map. He is seeking whom he can devour . . . Don't let it be you! Sin is the devil and sin is death. So choose life . . . choose Christ.

I don't know it all nor have I traveled the world in eighty days

I thank the Lord for allowing me to look back over my life, take an inventory, see where I went wrong when I was told to go right, and how I ended up. During a time in my life of wanting to be grown before my time my mother would always say to me "you think you are right all the time, you don't know everything." Yes, I realized later that some of the things that she told me made sense. Some things possibly could have been avoided or had a lesser impact if I had only listened. For instance, I was in a situation of walking off a job because I did not like what was being said to me by my supervisor. Keep in mind this was my first job of many and that was my attitude. I was taught that there are times when you have to be quiet . . . you will learn more. Life will teach us that some things are better left unsaid. I had to learn the hard way. I spoke too soon and the supervisor of my first job said "your services are no longer needed here." All this is saying is learn to take a little because it prepares us for tougher things to come. This is food for thought: Choose your battles wisely . . . they are not ours, they belong to the Lord.

How can you say you have my back

If you take a look at your surroundings you will find not all things look the same including the people that say they have your back. How can you say you have my back . . .

> . . . when I was down you stepped on me
> . . . when I had no shelter you allowed it to rain on my head
> . . . when I couldn't breathe and you were with oxygen and gave me none
> . . . when I thirst you had water and offered me none
> . . . when I was without a job and instead of looking for me you ran from me
> . . . when my vehicle was not operating you saw me at the bus stop blew your horn and kept it moving
> . . . when I went to jail you forgot all about me
> . . . when I left you a voicemail, you erased it
> . . . when you didn't have a girlfriend we were down like four flats and now that she has given you air you float off into the sunset as if I am just a glare in your rear view mirror

See, we must understand that life is like history, it repeats itself. The same people you meet going up you will meet on your way down. Hopefully they don't have the same heart or mindset as you. So many of us are stagnated because of the crab in the bucket mentality. We want to make it all about us, as if we've arrived and how can we when the engine is on and the vehicle is still moving. The Bible tells us to humble ourselves and display humility towards one another. This is food for thought: I shouldn't have to always say I have your back if I'm always proving it to you. Your talk should always reflect your walk

I am me

When I say I am me that's exactly what I mean. There is a tendency for most people to attempt to redefine who they are as they change. As for myself I have the tendency to redefine myself as a stream of events that God allowed to happen in my life which caused change in me. Primarily, I found that one of the roots of this tendency is when I recall both of my parents telling me from an early age to make something of myself which I can be proud of. After carefully searching deep within, the mental thought surfaced that I have an ego that needed to be named. I named that ego "Mark", due to the small element of innocence I have stored in the corner pocket of my brain to try and limit that which is limitless or infinite. This is the reason why most are unable to accept the concept of an infinite being, which is impossible for my mind to grasp.

I am me . . .

> because I have set boundaries for myself
> because I am a separation from my divinity
> because of my infinity
> because of the small element of innocence I have stored away
> because of the discovery of rules and parameters in my life
> because I allow change to be continual

. . . because of my new limited perception of who I am each time God allows an event to surface in my life that causes change and for that alone is why I am me. This is food for thought: I am me, I am me, I am me, and I will continue to be me.

Favor

I am more than sure we have all heard it before . . . that favor isn't fair. Favor is defined as an act of kindness beyond what is due or usual. On the other hand it is also defined as an act performed out of good will, generosity, or mercy. To me when it comes to God, He always show us acts of kindness and favor beyond what we are due . . . He allow us to live another day, He holds it down for us, gives us strength to cope, and He even allowed some of us to move to the front of the line when we know we should be in the back. Now, in various situations people show us favor, life has shown us favor, family has shown us favor, and the minister of the body of Christ we belong to or are affiliated with at some time or another has shown us favor. Believe it or not it still was God's doing.

It's funny how when things get rough many of us get in our feelings and get bent all out of shape, like when the minister isn't screaming your name anymore, you're not called on to do things anymore, you're not invited to their homes to eat anymore, the supervisor at work stopped giving you a head start over everyone else, the friend at the oil shop stopped allowing you to utilize their discount, or you cannot have this and you cannot have that. Stop! Take a look at yourself and take inventory: What role did you play? Maybe the season has changed or maybe you took advantage of what God has done and totally disregarded what He required you to do in order to maintain or keep permanent favor. This is food for thought: If we are living right according to God's word, then we must adjust to the season we're in.

Express yourself

Expressing yourself means to show other people your personality, to open up, to make your thoughts generally known, and heard to do what you want to do. I feel that because you are designed by God, an impartation in this earth, you can't be denied. So don't waste time attempting to get acceptance from people. People can be compared to so many things that make sense and then again things that don't make sense. For instance some men don't like tall women and they have no authority to change her height. Some women don't like short men and they don't have authority to change his. All I am saying is that I highly respect people who are not afraid to say what is on their mind and in their hearts. They express themselves, not afraid of letting others know who they are, and will let it be known that they are in control of themselves. This is food for thought: Express yourself! Tell the world that you are who God says you are and He gave you the authority to express yourself, don't go for second best, and put your own self to the test. Express yourself!.

No more drama

I am sure we agree that drama means an exciting, emotional, or unexpected series of events or set of circumstances. Yes, if you are living in the same world that I am, breathing the same air I am, and running into some miserable people then you surely can identify with drama. There are some who are designed to bring the drama into your life, if you allow them. They are the ones who have done everything you have, traveled every place you have, had the same car as you but purchased a better one, have the same set of shoes but paid a higher price for theirs, and the list can go on. This is one hundred and fifty-one percent drama. I shut down the drama by saying "don't start none won't be none". Keeping my tone and emotions intact, allowing the dramatic one to hear themselves talk, providing the dramatic one with positive feedback by answering with one-liners, such as "great", and ending it with "I am excited by all the things you've done and all the places you've been. However, I have a lot on my plate and at this time I have no room to fit anyone or anything else in. I tell you what, I have your number and I will give you a call when I am not so busy." This is food for thought: Shut the door on the drama and push forward with a clear mind and a clear heart. You have the authority to set the atmosphere. Therefore, no more drama! God knows where the story ends for me and while He is working on me, I pray that you will allow Him to work on you.

Sometimes it is best to just turn and walk away

We all know that no two individuals think alike or even process things the same way mentally or emotionally. If we've come to a point where we cannot seem to agree on anything then we should act as adults, speak as adults, explain our point of view as adults, and come to a place where we can maybe agree to disagree and move on. However, If this is impossible and we've gotten to where we're shouting at each other, blaming each other, not taking responsibility for our faults, and maybe even coming close to physical blows, then I would turn away to prevent wrath, I would walk away to keep from becoming physical, I would go in peace because violence is not me, and I would analyze what it is that I had done to allow the devil to almost destroy what was once a great friendship. This prevents me from saying things to you that I don't mean, from not ever wanting to befriend you, and stops me from thinking that if it is really this bad then maybe the friendship we had was not real to begin with. I must take the high road because it is right and the classy thing to do which displays growth and development within me. But on the other hand if you keep coming at me in a manner that violates my space and totally disrespects me then I must turn and walk away, not because I am weak or afraid but because I am practicing what I preach by working on me. However, you cannot continue to violate me. I am human and I will allow you to hang yourself. This is food for thought: Choose your battles wisely! If you "wisely" choose to rumble with me then I will and shall love you from afar. "Vengeance is mine," said the Lord. He can punish you a lot better and quicker than I can.

Dear Readers,

Those of you who purchased this book I say "thank you" for being a loyal supporter of mine. However, I pray that this book changes your views on the way you handle specific situations, the way you think, the way you mentally process things, your approach in defending yourself, confirmation that you are meek and not weak because you chose to walk away, power in knowing that you are only human, the ability to know we all are a work in progress with no exemptions, the gaining of additional knowledge pertaining to the way you love and respect others, and definitely the way you pick and choose your friends wisely. Remember, God is the One we all have to answer to for our actions. Therefore, come and let us all reason together in making this world a better place if we are willing to do so by imparting what we learned in working toward being on the straight and narrow. In closing, we all must reach back, grab one, teach one, encourage one, educate one, save one, and save ourselves.

Blessings to you,
Michael L. Jordan
Love you 4 Eternity

Peace
Love
Respect
And
Happiness

This book is dedicated to Kevin and Calvin Jordan and also in memory of my loving mother "Ruby L. Mason".

Printed in the United States
By Bookmasters